# Edexcel GCSE (9-1) Busine

## Theme 1: Investigating sm

## About you

Name: _____

Class: _____

Teacher(s): _____

Lessons: _____

# Contents

## Theme 1: Investigating small businesses

### Topic 1.1 Enterprise and entrepreneurship
1.1.1 The dynamic nature of business ..................................5
1.1.2 Risk and reward..........................................................8
1.1.3 The role of business enterprise................................13

### Topic 1.2 Spotting a business opportunity
1.2.1 Customer needs ........................................................17
1.2.2 Market research ........................................................21
1.2.3 Market segmentation................................................29
1.1.4 The competitive environment..................................34

### Topic 1.3 Putting a business idea into practice
1.1.1 Business aims and objectives ..................................38
1.1.2 Business revenues, costs and profits ......................43
1.1.3 Cash and cash-flow...................................................51
1.1.4 Sources of business finance ....................................56

### Topic 1.4 Making the business effective
1.4.1 The options for start-up and small businesses .....61
1.4.2 Business location ......................................................66
1.4.3 The marketing mix....................................................71
1.4.4 Business plans...........................................................76

### Topic 1.5 Understanding external influences on business
1.5.1 Business stakeholders..............................................80
1.5.2 Technology and business........................................84
1.5.3 Legislation and business..........................................91
1.5.4 The economy and business.....................................96
1.5.5 External influences..................................................101

## 1.1.1 The dynamic nature of business

**What you need to learn**
- Why new business ideas come about:
  - changes in technology
  - changes in what consumers want
  - products and services becoming obsolete
- How new business ideas come about:
  - original ideas
  - adapting existing products/services/ideas

A business is any organisation that trades in goods or services, normally with an aim to make a profit. These can be small e.g. a market stall selling fruit and vegetables; all the way up to large multinational businesses that operate across the world e.g. Coca Cola. At some point all businesses were a new idea by an entrepreneur.

### Why do new ideas come about?

New business ideas come from a range of sources. These include:

| Changes in technology | <ul><li>This could make an idea possible e.g. to sell goods online, develop an app or to promote the products of the business</li><li>New technology can create a need for supporting services or accessories e.g. web training or mobile phone covers</li><li>Technological innovations e.g. fitness trackers or software allow for innovation and improve the quality of the product</li></ul> |
|---|---|
| Changes in what consumers want | <ul><li>Changing tastes e.g. healthy drinks mean that there is a gap in the market</li><li>New trends e.g. fidget spinners or retro clothes lead to increased demand for products that can meet needs and wants</li><li>Changing demographics e.g. ageing population or tastes of different nationalities moving to the UK</li></ul> |

| | |
|---|---|
| Products and services becoming obsolete | • Obsolete means that the product has become out of date<br>• Better ways of doing things are discovered e.g. the tablet device to replace a typewriter<br>• Innovations change needs e.g. artificial turf or the bagless vacuum cleaner |

## How do new ideas come about?

| | |
|---|---|
| Original ideas | • Brainstorming is the process of asking a range of people to contribute ideas to a discussion. This leads to a large number of ideas encouraging creativity<br>• An entrepreneur may recognise a problem that exists either for themselves or others. This can generate a new business idea by finding a solution to that problem. Indeed, many businesses are created because most people have the same issues that need to be addressed<br>• Identifying a gap in the market, perhaps through an understanding that customer needs and wants are not being met<br>• Innovation of a concept or an existing product that can be adapted to meet needs and wants in the market |
| Adapting existing ideas | • Improving a good or service in order to meet the demands of the market<br>• Adapting to a new market<br>   • Importing a successful idea from abroad<br>   • Exporting a successful product to foreign markets |

## Test Yourself

### 1.1.1 The dynamic nature of business

1. What is a business?

2. What is meant by the term dynamic?

3. Give one example of a small business in your local area.

4. Give one example of a multinational business.

5. Explain why changes in technology can lead to new business ideas.

6. Explain why changes in what consumers want can lead to new business ideas.

7. Explain why products becoming obsolete can lead to new business ideas.

8. Explain how original ideas can lead to new business ideas.

9. Explain how adapting existing products can lead to new business ideas.

10. Give one example of a new idea and explain whether it has come from an original idea or the adaptation of an existing idea.

## 1.1.2 Risk and reward

**What you need to learn**
- The impact of risk and reward on business activity:
  - risk: business failure, financial loss, lack of security
  - reward: business success, profit, independence

An entrepreneur is someone who has an idea for a new venture and is willing to take a risk to set up a business. One of the commonly named characteristics of an entrepreneur is that they are risk-takers. There are a number of risks that can be associated with business activity. These include:
- business failure i.e. when a business ceases trading
- financial loss i.e. the entrepreneur and/or investors lose the capital they have invested in the business
- lack of security i.e. the loss of a guaranteed, regular income or return on investment

| | Risks |
|---|---|
| | **Business failure** |
| Failing to understand the market | Market research might be inadequate, meaning that the entrepreneur does not understand the market e.g. size and growth. Wrong segment is targeted, leading to a lack of demand for the product. Underestimating the degree and relative power of competition, particularly in competitive markets. |
| Poor planning | Inaccurate cash-flow forecasts might mean that the business is unable to finance day to day expenses. Inadequate resources might mean that the business is incapable of undertaking day to day business activities. |
| Poor decision making | Management inefficiency means that poor judgement has taken place in running the business, this may be particularly important if the entrepreneur is inexperienced. Lack of innovation means that the business is unable to adapt to the requirements of the market. |

| | |
|---|---|
| Badly organised | Poor stock control so that the business can't meet demand.<br>Inefficient labour means that the workforce is unable to fulfil their job role effectively.<br>Bad customer service can lead to a poor reputation and a lack of repeat custom.<br>Cash-flow/liquidity problems can lead to a lack of finance to meet day to day expenses e.g. to pay suppliers and the workforce. |
| Overtrading | Taking on too much work leading to the business gaining a bad reputation for poor quality and time management. |
| Non-viable idea in the first place! | Many ideas are not researched appropriately, and it is only a matter of time before the business fails. |

### Financial loss

| | |
|---|---|
| Unlimited liability | The owner may lose their personal belongings e.g. home and cars, if the value of these is needed to cover the debts of the business. This is particularly the case for smaller businesses such as sole traders that will have unlimited liability. |
| Limited liability | Although other investors face a financial risk, limited liability will protect against losing anything above the amount invested or promised. |
| Opportunity cost | There is also an opportunity cost with starting and running a business. The individual could have earned a wage in alternative employment. |

### Lack of security

| | |
|---|---|
| Financial security | The loss of a wage from alternative employment. The business is not guaranteed to be successful, leading to financial insecurity. The business owner might have to use their personal savings or borrow money to cover negative cash flows. |
| Personal security | The business is also a very emotional issue for the entrepreneur. They will tend to put greater time and effort into their work in order for it to succeed. This leads to stress and could ultimately lead to health problems. |

Despite the many risks associated with setting up a new business many people are willing to take these risks. This is because they believe they can make the business venture successful and therefore reap the rewards. These rewards include:
- business success i.e. when a business becomes established and is able to meet its objectives
- profit i.e. the ability to earn enough revenue to cover total costs and leave a surplus
- independence i.e. the ability of the entrepreneur to support themselves and their family from income earned from the business either as a salary or in drawings/dividends

| Reward | |
|---|---|
| **Business success** | |
| An ability to understand the market | Market research can lead to an entrepreneur having a better understanding of the target market.<br>Experience leads to improved decision-making, as the entrepreneur learns from past mistakes and successes.<br>Finding a niche, or gap, in the market allows the business to provide a product that is in demand but under provided. |
| Good planning | Cash-flow forecasts allow a business to anticipate future cash shortages, meaning it can put measures in place to improve liquidity.<br>Investment in appropriate resources will enhance the quality of product and the standard of service delivered.<br>A well-researched and thought out business plan can help guide an entrepreneur in the setting up and running of the business. |
| Good decision making | A strong business idea can stand out in competitive markets, giving the business a competitive advantage.<br>Innovation of products allows the business to adapt to changing needs.<br>Effective management of resources will lead to a better quality product and enhanced reputation. |

| | |
|---|---|
| Well organised | Good stock control ensures that demand is met, and waste is reduced.<br>Effective and well-trained employees can earn the business a reputation for quality.<br>Good customer service will lead to repeat custom. |
| Financial efficiency | Good cash flow management helps the business to remain liquid and reduce costs.<br>Budgeting will provide a target to aim at and help motivate workers within the business. |
| Luck! | Often the entrepreneur is in the right place at the right time. However, they still needed to take the risk of starting the business in the first place. |

## Profit

| | |
|---|---|
| Excess of revenue over total costs | As the business becomes established it is more likely that profits will increase. This is due to increased understanding of the market and brand awareness.<br>Business owners are likely to work harder as profits will benefit them directly.<br>Entrepreneurs may believe that the financial rewards of setting up a business will be significantly higher than the remuneration they receive in paid employment. |

## Independence

| | |
|---|---|
| Being your own boss leads to independence | A personal challenge and greater satisfaction.<br>Meeting self-esteem needs.<br>Helping provide employment for oneself and others, perhaps including family members.<br>Security for family, potentially leaving a legacy of a family business.<br>Not having to take instructions from others. |

# Test Yourself

## 1.1.2 Risk and reward

1. What is meant by the term entrepreneur?

2. What is meant by the term risk?

3. What is meant by the term reward?

4. Explain one reason why business failure is a risk to an entrepreneur.

5. Explain one reason why financial loss is a risk to an entrepreneur.

6. Explain one reason why loss of security is a risk to an entrepreneur.

7. Explain one reason why business success is a reward for an entrepreneur.

8. Explain one reason why profit acts as a reward for an entrepreneur.

9. Explain one reason why independence is a reward for an entrepreneur.

10. State two reasons why a new business may fail.

## 1.1.3 The role of business enterprise

**What you need to learn**
- The role of business enterprise and the purpose of business activity:
  - to produce goods or services
  - to meet customer needs
  - to add value: convenience, branding, quality, design, unique selling points.

The role of entrepreneurship:
  - an entrepreneur: organises resources, makes business decisions, takes risks

**The role of business enterprise and the purpose of business activity.**

A **business** provides **goods** or **services** to people, often in exchange for money.

**Products** are either goods or services.

A **good** is tangible e.g. cars, tables and pens.

A **service** is intangible i.e. you cannot touch it e.g. teaching and banking.

**Can you name a local business that provides goods?**
**Can you name a local business that provides services?**

There are a number of **reasons why businesses are set up**:
- To produce goods for sale
- To supply services for sale
- To distribute products to people
- To fulfil a business opportunity
- To provide a good or service that will benefit society

Businesses meet the **needs** and **wants** of consumers and other businesses.

Edexcel GCSE (9-1) Business Theme 1

A **need** is a good or service that is essential to survival e.g. food, shelter, and healthcare.

A **want** is something that is desired but is not essential e.g. new trainers or iPhone.

**Can you name a local business that provides for a need?**
**Can you name a local business that provides for a want?**

## Adding value

A business seeks to add value by improving the worth of inputs into the production process. This will allow it to charge more than it costs to produce a good or service.

The business can add value in a variety of ways:

- Convenience - selling a product that makes life easier for the customer, saving time and improving quality when people have busy lifestyles
- Branding - creating an identity for the business that distinguishes it and its products from other businesses. This can add value to a product allowing the business to charge higher prices
- Quality - creating a product that meets or exceeds customer expectations. This will lead to a good reputation and repeat custom
- Design - creating a product that is functional i.e. it achieves the purpose that it was bought for or aesthetically pleasing e.g. it looks good
- Unique selling point (USP) - creating a feature or characteristic within a brand that makes it stand out. This could be a logo or brand name e.g. Superdry, different ingredients e.g. SuperJam is sweetened by natural grape juice not sugar or product features e.g. Ford cars developed a heated front window

**Enterprise** is the formation of a new business or development of a new good or service to be introduced to the market.

An **entrepreneur** is a person who, having generated a new business idea, develops it by setting up a business.

*Mandy Habermann invented the Anywayup Cup after seeing a toddler leave juice stains on a cream coloured carpet – she invented a cup that did not spill by only releasing liquid when a child drank from it.*

The characteristics of an entrepreneur include:

- Organises resources – setting up a business is a complex task which can involve working with a range of people e.g. accountants and web designers as well as a range of resources e.g. finance and materials. Therefore, it is important that the entrepreneur is organised to ensure that this is managed effectively, and deadlines are met
- Makes business decisions – these might be **tactical** or short-term e.g. a restaurant deciding what to put on a menu or **strategic** or longer-term e.g. deciding to target a new market abroad
- Takes risks – new businesses often fail. An entrepreneur may be risking their time, finances and reputation when setting up a new business with no guarantee of success.

## Test Yourself

**1.1.3 The role of business enterprise**

1. With the use of an appropriate example, explain the difference between a good and a service.

2. What is the purpose of business activity?

3. What is a USP?

4. What is added value?

5. Explain one reason why convenience adds value to a product.

6. Explain one reason why branding adds value to a product.

7. Explain one reason why design adds value to a product.

8. What is an entrepreneur?

9. What is enterprise?

10. Outline three characteristics of an entrepreneur.

## 1.2.1 Customer needs

### What you need to learn
- Identifying and understanding customer needs:
  - what customer needs are: price, quality, choice, convenience
  - the importance of identifying and understanding customers: generating sales, business survival

Identifying and understanding customer needs to achieve a profit.
- Customer needs are:
  - Identified by carrying out market research
  - Satisfied by an integrated marketing mix
  - Revisited by on-going research and relevant changes to the marketing mix

**What customer needs are**

**Price** is the amount that the customer has to pay to receive the good or service. Businesses use different pricing strategies to price their products, taking into account a number of factors such as market research, competitors' prices and the state of the economy. If there is plenty of competition price becomes more important to a business. Potential customers can shop around, meaning that businesses are more sensitive to the price that competitors charge. Some businesses have little competition. For example, a pharmaceuticals business might have a patent on its product, stopping other businesses from producing it.

Price comparison websites have made it easier for customers to shop around to find the best price.

**Quality** is about meeting the expectations of the customer. If these are met, then the business has satisfied customer needs. For example, McDonalds customers do not expect a fine dining experience. They expect fast service, with a standardised product at a reasonable price. No matter where the restaurant, the expectation is always the same. Restaurants are easily accessible and open at convenient times, such as breakfast. One would expect friendly staff, but knowledge of the product sold is not so important. For a product with better ingredients, such as an Argentinian steak house, the customer is prepared to pay more. This means that prices are higher, but one would expect better customer service. Understanding of the product sold will be more important, including how to cook the steak and what side dishes are suitable.

*At fresh food chain Pret a Manger staff are monitored to make sure they are "relentlessly cheerful" when dealing with customers. Mystery shoppers visit stores every week to check that all staff are displaying 'Pret perfect' behaviour. The business says that all staff must be 'charming', 'have presence' and create a 'sense of fun'. Workers should not 'annoy people' or be 'moody' or 'bad-tempered'. If the mystery shopper gives a branch a positive report the whole team gets a bonus. If the report is bad the whole team misses out on the bonus.*

**Choice** is important as different customers have different tastes. For example, meat products might be distinguished between low fat, standard or Halal. Some customers might prefer a vegetarian version, whilst others look for a vegan alternative. Businesses must take into account the diverse range of products that consumers are looking to buy. Some businesses, such as Amazon, have been highly successful by offering a huge choice of products, such as books. Other businesses, such as Asda, restrict their choice of books to best sellers. This suggests that one reason for Amazon's success is its large product range. Whereas Asda provide a different need, in that they offer a smaller range of high demand products.

**Convenience** has become more important as lifestyles have changed. People are less willing to wait for a product to be delivered, particularly as they have busy lives.
This can take a variety of forms, including:
- Ease of access to the product e.g. car parking or home delivery
- The time taken to receive the product
- Store opening hours e.g. 24 hour service

The internet has made it easier to order products and firms have improved distribution methods to ensure that customers receive the product as quickly and conveniently as possible.

It is important to research the market to identify its customers and their needs. Failure to do this would result in an inability to compete or make a profit.

Identifying and understanding customer wants and needs is important in order to:
- Provide a good or service that customers will buy
  - If there is no demand the business will not survive
- Generate sales
  - Meeting needs will attract new customers and help maintain existing customers

*In 1985 Coca-Cola announced that it was to change the ingredients of its established and well-loved drink in favour of a new recipe, quickly labelled as 'New Coke'. This was a response to the surge in sales of its main competitor, Pepsi Cola. However, the change backfired, as protest groups across the US campaigned to get their product back. Upsetting fiercely loyal customers was not the intention of the business. After 77 days it backed down and reintroduced the old recipe, under the name Classic Coca-Cola, whilst still producing the new recipe under the label Coke II. More recently in 2016 Cadbury's saw the sales of its Creme Eggs' fall by £6m when it tried to reduce costs by switching the Dairy Milk shell for a cheaper chocolate.*

**Has a change in a product that you buy led to dissatisfied customers?**

Edexcel GCSE (9-1) Business Theme 1

# Test Yourself

## 1.2.1 Spotting a business opportunity

1. What are customer needs?

2. Distinguish between identifying and understanding customer needs.

3. Explain one reason why the price of a product is important in meeting customer needs.

4. Explain one reason why the quality of a product is important in meeting customer needs.

5. Explain one reason why having a range of products is important in meeting customer needs.

6. Explain one reason why convenience is important in meeting customer needs.

7. State one business that competes on price.

8. State one business that competes on quality.

9. Explain one reason why identifying and understanding customer needs can generate sales.

10. Explain one reason why identifying and understanding customer needs can help a business survive.

## 1.2.2 Market research

**What you need to learn**
- The purpose of market research:
  - to identify and understand customer needs
  - to identify gaps in the market
  - to reduce risk
  - to inform business decisions
- Methods of market research:
  - primary research: survey, questionnaire, focus group, observation
  - secondary research: internet, market reports, government reports
- The use of data in market research:
  - qualitative and quantitative data
  - the role of social media in collecting market research data
  - the importance of the reliability of market research data

### The purpose of market research

Market research is the collection and analysis of data and information to inform a business about its market.
- Market research will help a business to understand:
  - Its customers' needs and wants
  - The competitors' actions and relative strengths or weaknesses
  - The market place i.e. size, spending habits and trends

Businesses therefore conduct market research in order to identify market opportunities and gain an insight into their customers and competitors.
- To identify and understand customers needs
  - Trends and patterns in buying behaviours
  - Likes and dislikes
  - Factors influencing choice
  - Attitudes to different elements of the marketing mix

- Identify gaps in the market
    - Assess what is currently in the market
    - Identify market opportunities
    - Develop new business ideas
    - Assess feasibility of filling gaps that have been identified
- To reduce risk
    - Providing an understanding of market trends
    - To gain insight into what products to produce in future in order to meet customer needs
- To inform business decisions
    - Trends and patterns in buying behaviours
    - Likes and dislikes of existing and potential customers
    - Factors influencing choice
    - Attitudes to different elements of the marketing mix

There are two categories of market research:
- **Primary market research** (field research) involves the collection of first hand data that did not exist before. Therefore it is original data
- **Secondary market research** (desk research) is research that has already been undertaken by another organisation and therefore already exists

|  | Primary | Secondary |
| --- | --- | --- |
| **Advantages** | Specific to the needs of the business<br>Up to date - new information<br>Can be quite cheap e.g. a focus group | Already collected so quick to access<br>May be from an expert source<br>Can provide a lot of information/data |
| **Disadvantages** | Time consuming<br>Likely to be relatively small scale and therefore lack accuracy<br>Not designed or collected by an expert | General research rather than specific to the business<br>Often have to pay for it – can be expensive<br>Presents past data |

Methods of primary market research include:
- Survey
- Questionnaire
- Focus group
- Observation

Methods of secondary market research include:
- Internet
- Market reports
- Government reports

|  | Definition | Explanation |
| --- | --- | --- |
| **Surveys** | The collection and analysis of aggregated data that is used to inform businesses. | Often information is taken from questionnaires. Primarily quantifiable research which can easily be analysed statistically. Often provides respondents with options to choose from. Can be postal, telephone, face-to-face or on-line. |
| **Questionnaires** | A set of questions, used to gather information that is given to an individual with a choice of answers. | May include open and closed questions, but primarily closed. A relatively easy way to collect consumer opinions. Normally paper based. |
| **Focus groups** | Groups of consumers who share their views and opinions in a focused discussion. | Provides qualitative data. Allows for follow up questions. Can be combined with viewing or trying a product or range of products e.g. taste tests. |

|  | Definition | Explanation |
|---|---|---|
| **Observation** | A method of collecting and analysing data from watching the actions of individuals in either natural or planned situations. | This may take a covert form where those being observed are unaware.<br>This allows businesses to understand consumer behaviour, particularly as individuals are in their natural environment.<br>It could be overt, where individuals realise that they are being watched. However, this means that individuals might modify behaviour. |
| **Internet** | Using information that already has been collected and is available on the internet. | Wide range of information freely available.<br>Can carry out research independently.<br>Examples include government reports and the census. |
| **Market reports** | An analysis of the conditions associated with a particular market e.g. the fashion industry. | Information can be available from a range of sources e.g. newspapers, trade journals, company reports, government statistics, educational papers and books.<br>The validity of information may need to be checked. |
| **Government reports** | Publications released by government organisations regarding a range of issues including demographics and the state of the economy. | These enable businesses to understand conditions in various markets and the economy as a whole.<br>Examples include national and local government reports e.g. those released by the Office for National Statistics (ONS). |

|  | Benefits | Drawbacks |
|---|---|---|
| **Surveys** | Cost effective. Quick and easy. Allow for a broad range of information. More in depth understanding. | May lead to bias. Often, dishonest answer. More prone to error by researcher. |
| **Questionnaire** | Cost effective. Quick and easy. Allow collection of data that can be analysed. | Does not allow for qualitative information. May lead to bias. Often, dishonest answers. |
| **Focus groups** | In depth understanding of personal and group opinions. Groups can work together to provide solutions. Range of specialisms. | Can be taken over by more dominant individuals. Dependent on the skills of interviewees and interviewer. Difficult to manage e.g. disagreements. |
| **Observation** | Allows greater insight into customer needs. Cheap and easy to undertake. | May be ethical concern regarding privacy, if covert. If overt, people might change their behaviour. Is open to interpretation. |
| **Internet research** | Cost effective. Allow collection of a range of data. Huge amount of information available. | Secondary research so not always specific. Difficult to find exact information. Overwhelming. |
| **Market reports** | Provides insight regarding trends in the market. Allows the business to understand the degree and quality of competition. Can help identify gaps in the market. | May not be specific enough for business requirements. Can become dated very quickly in dynamic markets. Often expensive to access. |

|  | Benefits | Drawbacks |
|---|---|---|
| Government reports | Provide insight regarding a range of information. Often free for businesses to access. Extensive coverage of factors that impact on businesses. | Not specific to business needs. Tend to have a broad focus. Huge amount of data might be seen as overwhelming. |

Fujitsu is a Japanese multinational corporation that specialises in providing IT services. It has 159 000 employees in over 100 countries. It particularly focuses on its relationships with key customers; clients tend to stay with the business for a long period of time. It uses focus groups on a regular basis to inform its market research. These are often informal, perhaps over breakfast or lunch. Fujitsu employees will have established close relations with their clients, allowing for an understanding of customer needs. Discussion will focus on ideas for new products or how existing products can be improved. This leads to in depth understanding of the problems that customers might face and allows Fujitsu to formulate a solution.

**How does using market research, such as focus groups, lead to increased sales for a business in the future?**

Market research can be quantitative or qualitative:

- **Quantitative market research** is numerical. The data collected is easy to analyse and represent graphically
- **Qualitative market research** is non numerical. It is about people's opinions

## The role of social media in collecting market research data

**Social media** is the use of the internet to create online communities. Increasingly, businesses use social media to gain insight into markets. It provides easy and cost effective access to customers and key players in the market.

Social media platforms, such as Twitter or Facebook, allow businesses to analyse trends, making their findings up-to-date. Businesses have social media departments that comb the internet gathering data that can be used to understand markets.

## The importance of the reliability of market research data
You need to be able to interpret and use qualitative and quantitative market research findings.
The validity of market research data can be questioned. Those undertaking the research might have ulterior motives, leading to bias in reports.

The quality of findings can also be questioned. Reports are only as good as the quality of research and access to information used to complete them.

## Test Yourself

### 1.2.2 Market research

1. What is market research?

2. Distinguish between primary and secondary market research.

3. State one advantage and one disadvantage of surveys as a method of market research.

4. State one advantage and one disadvantage of questionnaires as a method of market research.

5. State one advantage and one disadvantage of focus groups as a method of market research.

6. State one advantage and one disadvantage of observations as a method of market research.

7. State one advantage and one disadvantage of market reports as a method of market research.

8. State one advantage and one disadvantage of government reports as a method of market research.

9. Distinguish between quantitative and qualitative market research.

10. Explain one reason why social media is useful for collecting market research data.

## 1.2.3 Market segmentation

**What you need to learn**
- How businesses use market segmentation to target customers:
  - identifying market segments: location, demographics, lifestyle, income, age
  - market mapping to identify a gap in the market and the competition

**Segmentation** groups customers into subsections of the market with similar characteristics.

Market segmentation divides the market into different sections (segments) to enable the business to specifically target customers with the most appropriate products.

This may be better for a business than the mass market approach that makes one product for all, because customers often differ in terms of:
- What they want
- How much they are able or willing to pay
- The amount of a good or service that they want
- How and where they buy
- What types of media they would encounter

Segmentation therefore allows a business to better target customers by meeting their needs more specifically. It allows the business to target a subsection with tailored goods or services.

Segmentation includes by:
- Location
- Demographics
- Lifestyle
- Income
- Age

| | |
|---|---|
| **Location** | This defines market categories based on where people live e.g. regions, cities or neighbourhoods.
People in different geographical areas display different characteristics.
For example, those in the South East are more affluent on average than those in Scotland. Therefore, a house builder may build more luxury, detached homes. |
| **Demographics** | This identifies subgroups of the population based on peoples' profiles or characteristics.
This might include age, gender, level of education, race, religion, family size or stage in life e.g. empty nesters.
Demographics look at the social and economic characteristics of individuals and households. |
| **Lifestyle** | This defines market categories based on the way that people live their lives.
It will look at the activities, interests and opinions (AIO) of individuals.
Businesses will customise products based on these.
Interests and hobbies can be identified, allowing businesses to be far more specific in identifying the target market. |
| **Income** | Targeting customers based on the amount of money they have at their disposal.
Income can have a direct influence on what customers are willing and able to buy.
Products can have higher added value to attract a more affluent market segment.
For example, shoe manufacturers may specialise in hand made leather shoes. |
| **Age** | Targeting a specific age group e.g. age 5-6.
This can include targeting a stage in the life cycle e.g. teenagers or empty nesters.
For example, a tour operator may offer coach holidays aimed at the over 60 market. |

Income segmentation sometimes makes use of socio-economic groups.

A – Higher managerial such as chief executives and chairmen
B – Intermediate managerial such as solicitors, accountants and doctors
C1 – Supervisory, clerical or junior professional such as teachers and junior managers
C2 – Skilled manual such as plumbers, electricians and carpenters
D – Semi and unskilled such as refuse collectors and window cleaners
E – Pensioners, casual workers, students and unemployed

There are a number of benefits for a business that uses segmentation:
- Products that more closely suit customer needs
  - By marketing products that appeal specifically to customers either at different stages of their life or with different incomes, a business can retain customers who might otherwise switch to other products or brands
- Target marketing communications
  - A business can identify the type of newspaper, magazine or TV programme that its chosen consumer would use and focus its attention on these. This saves the business' resources
- The ability to dominate within a segment
  - For smaller businesses this enables them to gain a foothold in a certain market. This can then become an ideal platform for growth

**Market mapping** can help a new or established business identify a gap in the market. It can see what segment of the market is underprovided for and look at producing a product to fill that gap. It also gives a business real insight into the competition within the same market as its own product.

A market map looks at 2 sets of opposites e.g. high price: low price v high quality: low quality.

It can look at a range of factors e.g.
- Quality
- Ease of use
- Ease of access (location)
- Speed (e.g. cars)
- Degree of innovation

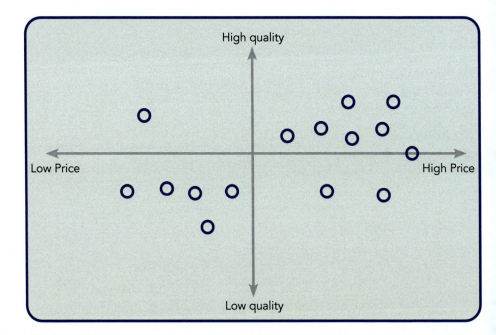

The market map shows that there are plenty of high quality, high priced products and plenty of low priced, low quality products. Therefore, there might be a gap for:
- high quality, low price
- low quality, high price
- very high quality, high price
- very low quality, low price

## Test Yourself

### 1.2.3 Market segmentation

1. What is segmentation?

2. What is demographic segmentation?

3. What is age segmentation?

4. What is location segmentation?

5. What is income segmentation?

6. Explain how segmentation allows a business to target customers.

7. State one additional benefit to a business of market segmentation.

8. What is meant by socio-economic groups?

9. What is a marketing map?

10. Draw a market map for the fashion industry plotting cheap: expensive against functional: fashionable.

## 1.2.4 The competitive environment

> **What you need to learn**
> - Understanding the competitive environment:
>   - strengths and weaknesses of competitors based on: price, quality, location, product range and customer service
>   - the impact of competition on business decision making

A **market** is the place where buyers and seller come together to exchange goods and services for money. This can be a physical location such as a shop or non-physical such as a web site.

**Competition** is the rivalry between businesses who operate in the same market. They try to be better than each other in order to gain customers, sales and profits. This can be achieved in a number of ways e.g. brand, unique product, better value for money. The type of competition in the market place varies between industries.

### Strengths and weaknesses of competitors based on:
**Price**
In mass markets businesses that can keep costs to a minimum have a distinct advantage. As they buy in bulk they can attain discounts. This reduces costs helping the business keep prices low. This will lead to lower prices and increased market share.

**Quality**
Some businesses compete on being highly differentiated with better quality products. This allows them to charge high prices. However, other businesses will benefit from producing lower quality but cheaper products.

## Location

Certain products require there to be a high footfall. These include service sector products such as restaurants where physical presence is important. For other businesses low cost is more important. This may be why some businesses relocate abroad to produce their goods.

*Many large businesses have relocated call centres abroad including big banks Barclays, HSBC and Santander. It is reported costs could be as much as 40% lower. However, customers have complained stating that they prefer the call centres to be based in the UK. Santander have listened to customer feedback and moved back to the UK. All of Santander UK's 1.5 million monthly customer service calls are now answered in the UK. The bank has created 500 call centre jobs in Glasgow, Leicester and Liverpool to absorb the calls that would have gone to Bangalore and Pune.*

## Product range

Some businesses will sell a large range of products, meaning that they can use their brand awareness to increase overall sales. As there is greater choice, this will attract more customers.

## Customer service

Good quality customer service will lead to a strong reputation, improving brand awareness. This will increase sales and repeat custom, leading to greater market share.

## The impact of competition on business decision making

If there are **lots of competitors** in a market this will increase the power of the consumers who will have a range of businesses that they can buy their products from. This will push down prices where goods are homogenous (the same) and no brand loyalty has been established.

If there are just a **few large competitors** in the market, competition tends to be in non-price terms and uses other elements of the marketing mix i.e. the product, promotion and place to gain a competitive advantage.

Competition impacts on businesses in a number of ways. These include:
- Price e.g. the need to lower prices to match those of competitors
- Promotional activity e.g. the need to increase the promotional budget in order to maintain existing customers or attract new customers
- Market share e.g. loss of sales forcing a business to change elements of the marketing mix
- Need to innovate e.g. bring out new products to attract customers
- Availability of skilled workers e.g. increase financial incentives to keep talented employees
- Location decisions e.g. move to premises that are higher cost but have a greater footfall
- Strategies for growth e.g. look to move into new markets, maybe abroad

If there is **only one business** selling a good or a service then it would be able to charge whatever price it wished, especially if the product is a need, as nobody else can provide this good. This is sometimes referred to as a monopoly.

A business may face no or minimal competition in the following circumstances:
- Niche market that requires very specialised goods or services
- Niche market that is too small to attract competition
- Geographical location targeting a small local market e.g. one fish and chip shop in a small village
- Market leader or dominant business that makes it difficult for others to enter the market
- Large outlay to establish a business, for example, need to lay cables to provide broadband
- Exclusive rights to a product, brand, licence or territory

# Test Yourself

## 1.2.4 The competitive environment

1. What is a market?

2. What is competition?

3. Explain why price can act as a strength for a business.

4. Explain why quality can act as a strength for a business.

5. Explain why location can act as a strength for a business.

6. Explain why product range can act as a strength for a business.

7. Explain why customer service can act as a strength for a business.

8. Explain one positive impact of competition on a business.

9. Explain one negative impact of competition on a business.

10. Explain one decision a business can make to reduce the level of competition it faces in a market.

## 1.3.1 Business aims and objectives

**What you need to learn**
- What business aims and business objectives are
- Business aims and objectives when starting up:
  - financial aims and objectives: survival, profit, sales, market share, financial security
  - non-financial aims and objectives: social objectives, personal satisfaction, challenge, independence and control
- Why aims and objectives differ between businesses

### What are business aims and objectives?

**Business aims and objectives** are the goals that a business wants to achieve.
Aims are general e.g. market growth.
Objectives are specific e.g. market growth of 5% in 2 years.

Business objectives will vary from one business to another e.g.
- a new business may want to survive in its first year
- a sandwich shop may want to gain 10% more customers
- An established business may want to enter new markets abroad

A business might set different aims for the short, medium and long term.

Business aims and objectives when starting up will include:

### Financial aims and objectives

- Survival: the ability of a business to continue to exist
- Profit: to achieve a surplus of revenue over costs
- Sales: to expand, maybe through more customers and branches, therefore increasing sales
- Market share: to increase the percentage of the total market that one brand or business owns
- Financial security: after it has established itself in the market a business will try to ensure that its cash flows are positive so that it can pay its day to day and long term bills

## Non-financial aims and objectives

- Social objectives: to do the morally correct thing, behaving in a way that is good for society
- Personal satisfaction: being successful helps to meet self-esteem needs
- Challenge: individuals want to test themselves to see if they can achieve their goals. Running an organisation is a real test of character, allowing the individual to see if they can accomplish what they set out to do
- Independence and control: the owner of an organisation has complete control of decision-making. This allows them to make decisions on product, location, pricing strategies and who to employ. Therefore, they can run the business as they see fit

*The Balloon Tree, a farm shop near York, has the following aims:*
- *"Fewer Food Miles – More Farm Yards"*
- *Ensure all produce is top quality*
- *Source everything locally*
- *Make the most of home grown produce*

**Can you match the aims of The Balloon Tree to the types of aims listed above?**

**Why set objectives?** Objectives can help in both the day to day running of a business and in measuring its performance.

**Purpose of setting objectives**
- Setting targets that the business can work towards
- These provide a clear focus for the business
- Measure actual performance against targets
- Objectives may change as the business changes

The role of objectives in running a business include:

- The use of corporate objectives to inform functional objectives. The corporate objective is what the business wants to achieve. This can then be broken down into functional objectives giving each department clear targets to work towards. This will ensure everyone is pulling in the same direction.
- To inform decision making. Each time a decision is made managers can ask "will this help us to achieve the objectives?"
- The objectives need to be communicated with all employees, giving everyone a sense of belonging and responsibility, to create motivation.
- Provides a quantifiable target against which businesses can monitor and assess performance.

The objectives set will differ between businesses. Possible reasons for this include:

| | |
|---|---|
| **Size of the business** | A small business may be happy to profit satisfice to keep a work life balance for its owners with no wish to grow. A big business may want to achieve further growth or increase market share. If the domestic market is saturated it may look to expand abroad. |
| **Level of competition faced** | In a highly competitive market a business may struggle to survive. In a market where there are a limited number of businesses they may all want to gain a competitive advantage and market share. |
| **Type of business** | A company may have an objective to maximise profits to increase shareholder value. A not-for-profit business will have social and ethical objectives. |

As a business grows it will still have many of the same objectives as it did when it was a small business. In addition, it might have new ones, such as:

- **Becoming the dominant business in the market**

A dominant business is one that has the highest market share.

There are a number of benefits in being the largest organisation, including:
- **Lack of competition** can help them to:
  - Develop and maintain customer loyalty
  - Restrict output and charge higher prices
- **Economies of scale** such as:
  - Bulk buying, reducing unit costs
  - Advertising, helping to develop brand image
- Use of its **financial resources** to maintain its position:
  - Predatory pricing, selling at a loss to price firms out of the market
  - Research and development, to produce new products

- **Expanding internationally**

An organisation that has achieved its growth objective in the UK might look to international markets in order to continue its growth. These can provide new markets for exports, increasing revenue and profit.

- **Ethical and environmental considerations**

Social costs and benefits are the costs and benefits to society created by the activities of a business. A business may want to take action to limit its social costs and maximise its social benefits.

## Using business objectives to measure success

| Business Objective | Use in measuring the success of a business |
| --- | --- |
| **Survival** | Has the business enough cash to meet day to day expenses? |
| **Profit** | How does the actual profit compare to the target for profit? |
| **Growth** | Has the business achieved growth e.g. increased sales or launched a new product? |
| **Market share** | What is the business' market share? How does this compare to competitors? |
| **Customer satisfaction** | What are customers saying? Is feedback positive? Are there many complaints? |
| **Ethical** | Has it kept its promises? Is it guilty of any unethical activities? |
| **Sustainable** | Are targets being met e.g. recycling, energy use, reducing waste? |

## Test Yourself

### 1.3.1 Business aims and objectives

1. What are business aims and objectives?

2. State two possible business aims for a start-up business.

3. State two possible business aims for a business that has been trading successfully for 3 years.

4. State and explain two benefits of setting business objectives.

5. Distinguish between financial and non-financial aims and objectives.

6. Explain how business objectives can be used to measure success.

7. State two stakeholders and explain how they can influence business objectives.

8. Explain how and why objectives will differ between businesses.

9. State a possible objective for a not-for-profit business.

10. What are ethical objectives?

## 1.3.2 Business revenues, costs and profits

**What you need to learn**
- The concept and calculation of:
  - revenue
  - fixed and variable costs
  - total costs
  - profit and loss
  - interest
  - break even level of output
  - margin of safety

- Interpretation of break even diagrams:
  - the impact of changes in revenue and costs
  - break even level of output
  - margin of safety
  - profit and loss

In business the word money can apply to lots of different things including **price**, **costs**, **revenue** and **profit**. It is therefore important you always use the correct **financial term**.

What are the **costs** of a business?

**Costs** = the expenses incurred by a business when providing goods or services

**e.g. rent of a garage forecourt, buckets, sponges, shampoo and wax.**

Some costs stay the same regardless of output e.g. rent on the garage forecourt, of £35.00 per day, has to be paid whether 1 car is washed or 100 cars. These are called **fixed costs**.

Some costs will change with the amount of output **e.g. the more cars washed the more shampoo and wax that is used, at £1.10 per car.** These are called **variable costs**.

Total costs are calculated as:
Total costs = Fixed cost + (Variable cost per unit x number of units)
or
Total cost = Fixed costs + total variable costs
e.g. £35.00 + (£1.10 x 24 cars) = £35.00 + £26.40 = £61.40

What is a business' **revenue**? How much does it **earn** from sales?

**Price** = the amount of money paid by a consumer for a good or service **e.g. a hand car wash is £5.00.**
**Sales** = the number of items sold **e.g. 24 car washes a day.**
**Revenue** = the total value of money being earned by the business from sales.
**Revenue is calculated as:**
Revenue = number of items sold x price
e.g. 24 car washes a day x £5.00
= £120.00 sales revenue per day

Remember in the exam you will need a calculator

Having considered both sides of the equation i.e. **costs** and **revenues** a business can now consider the **relationship between them**.

How does a business know if it has made a **profit** or a **loss**?

**Profit or Loss** = the difference between revenue and costs.
If **revenue** is **greater** than **costs** the business has made a profit.

**Profit is calculated as:**
Revenue – total costs
e.g. Revenue £120.00 – total costs £61.40 = Profit £58.60 per day
If the business opened for 320 days a year total profit would be £58.60 x 320 = £18 752

# Relationships between prices, costs, revenues and profits

A business that wants to **increase profit** has two options:
- Increase revenue e.g.
  - change price to sell more
  - improve product or customer service to attract more customers
  - increase promotion, as long as the cost of the promotion isn't higher than the extra revenue gained
- Reduce costs e.g.
  - find cheaper raw materials, but be careful not to affect quality
  - reduce staff hours
  - introduce new technology to reduce costs in the long run
- or a third option – a bit of both!

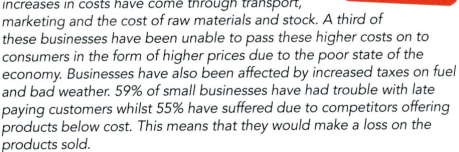

**Rising costs at small businesses** - *According to a survey by the Forum of Private Business the majority of small businesses have seen an increase in their business costs in recent years. Rising energy prices have hit 85% of these businesses. Other major increases in costs have come through transport, marketing and the cost of raw materials and stock. A third of these businesses have been unable to pass these higher costs on to consumers in the form of higher prices due to the poor state of the economy. Businesses have also been affected by increased taxes on fuel and bad weather. 59% of small businesses have had trouble with late paying customers whilst 55% have suffered due to competitors offering products below cost. This means that they would make a loss on the products sold.*

Interest is the reward for saving or the price of borrowing. Interest payments place pressure on the cash flow of a business. However, many entrepreneurs use bank loans as an important source of finance to start-up, run and expand a business.

**Interest (on loans)** can be calculated using the formula:

Interest (on loans) =

$$\frac{\text{Total repayment} - \text{borrowed amount}}{\text{Borrowed amount}} \times 100$$

**Worked example:**
A business takes out a loan for **£10 000**. They will have to pay back **£12 000** over 3 years.

The interest on the loan is:
£12 000 - £10 000/£10 000 × 100
= £2 000/£10 000 × 100
= **20%**


**Break-even output** is the level of output, expressed in units, where a business is not making a profit or a loss.
At this point total revenues (TR) = total costs (TC).
Each time an item is sold the difference between selling price and the variable cost is contributed towards, paying first the fixed costs and then contributing towards the profit.

Break-even output can be illustrated using a break-even chart. A **break-even chart** is a graphical representation of a business' costs and revenues at different levels of output. This allows it to identify:
- the profit or loss at different levels of output
- the break-even level of output
- the margin of safety

Break-even chart:
- Break-even point is read in units off the horizontal axis
- Can be used to read the loss or profit of a business at given levels of output by calculating the difference between the total cost and total revenue on the vertical axis

**Margin of safety** is the difference between the actual level of output and the break-even level of output.

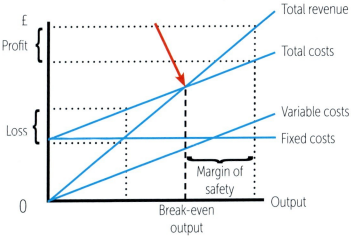

Changes in revenues or costs will impact on both the break-even level of output and the margin of safety. Changes in revenue will be shown by the curve becoming more or less steep. The total revenue curve will always start at 0. The diagram below shows the impact of a fall in revenue.

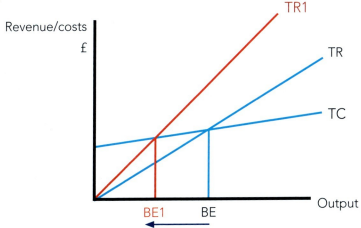

Changes in costs will be shown by a movement of the total cost curve:
- If fixed costs change the TC curve will shift parallel to the old curve
- If variable costs change then the TC curve will become more or less steep but will still start at the same point i.e. the start of the fixed costs curve

The diagram below shows the impact of a fall in fixed costs.

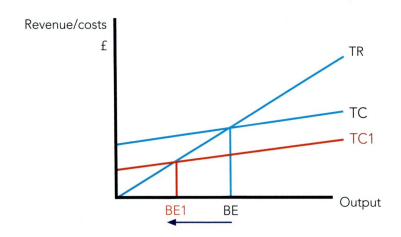

The diagram below shows the impact of a rise in variable costs

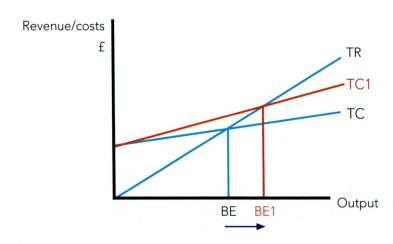

The table below shows the impact of changes to revenue and costs on break even, margin of safety and profit.

|  | Break even | Margin of safety | Profit |
|---|---|---|---|
| Costs go up | ↑ | ↓ | ↓ |
| Costs go down | ↓ | ↑ | ↑ |
| Revenue goes up | ↓ | ↑ | ↑ |
| Revenue goes down | ↑ | ↓ | ↓ |

| Advantages of break-even | Disadvantages of break-even |
|---|---|
| Allows businesses to calculate the minimum number of sales needed to make a profit and therefore helps assess the feasibility of an enterprise.<br><br>Can predict the outcome if variables such as cost or price change.<br><br>Provides a target.<br><br>Helps inform decision making.<br><br>An important part of a business plan which may help an entrepreneur secure finance. | Based on predicted costs and revenues.<br><br>Ignores any purchasing economies of scale that might be gained e.g. discounts for buying in bulk.<br><br>Only shows how many sales are needed. It doesn't do anything towards achieving them.<br><br>New entrepreneurs will find it difficult to accurately predict costs or revenues. |

# Test Yourself

**1.3.2 Business revenues, costs and profits**

1. What are fixed costs?

2. What are variable costs?

3. What are total costs?

4. What are revenues?

5. What is the formula for calculating profit or loss?

6. What is the break-even level of output?

7. What is the margin of safety?

8. What is the formula for interest (on loans)?

9. A business has made a profit of £35 000. Its revenue is £70 000 and total variable costs are £15 000. What are its fixed costs?

10. A business has an output of 90 000 units. Its break point is 75 000 units. What is its margin of safety?

## 1.3.3 Cash and cash-flow

### What you need to learn
- The importance of cash to a business:
  - to pay suppliers, overheads and employees
  - to prevent business failure (insolvency)
  - the difference between cash and profit
- Calculation and interpretation of cash-flow forecasts:
  - cash inflows
  - cash outflows
  - net cash flow
  - opening and closing balances

Cash is important to a business. Without cash it cannot survive in the medium to long run. This will lead to business failure (insolvency).

Without cash it cannot:
- Pay suppliers, overheads and employees
- Buy new raw materials or stock
- Pay workers
- Operate machinery
- Market its products

Cash flow problems exist when a business has a negative cash balance at the end of a period e.g. a month.

**Cash flow** is the **movement** of **money in (income/receipts)** and **money out (expenses/payments)** of a business.

**Cash flow forecasts** are used to help understand the flow of **cash in** and **cash out** of the business as well as whether the **closing balance** (the balance at the end of a month) will be positive or negative.

## The importance of cash flow forecasts

Businesses normally produce a forecast of their expected cash flow before the start of the year. This allows the business to spot any **potential cash shortfalls** in advance by identifying **negative closing balances**. The business can then either:
- Look to avoid the negative closing balances or
- Make plans e.g. a prearranged overdraft

The business can monitor **actual cash flow** against **predicted cash flow**.

The business can also identify **positive closing balances** to see if too much cash is sat dormant when it could be used to grow the business or earn a higher rate of interest.

A negative closing balance on a cash flow could lead to business failure (insolvency).

## Consequences of cash flow problems

Cash shortages can lead to the inability to meet **day to day expenses** e.g. buy stock and pay wages. The business may therefore have to **sell assets** to pay expenses. Failure to cover debts can result in the business going into **receivership** and **closing down**.

**Receivership** is when an organisation **takes control of all the assets** of a failing business and turns them into cash to try **and pay off the business' debts**. The business ceases to exist.

## Net cash flow

The difference between total cash in and total cash out.

e.g. Total cash in     =   £2 000
     Total cash out    =   £1 400
     Net cash flow     =   £600

i.e. £600 more has flowed into the business than has flowed out

# Example of a cash flow statement

|  | Jan (£) | Feb (£) | Mar (£) | Apr (£) | Calculations |
|---|---|---|---|---|---|
| **Income** | | | | | |
| Sales | 4 000 | 4 500 | 5 500 | 6 500 | |
| **Total income** | 4 000 | 4 500 | 5 500 | 6 500 | Add all incomes together |
| **Expenses** | | | | | |
| Materials | 800 | 900 | 1 000 | 1 200 | |
| Wages & salaries | 1 000 | 1 000 | 1 200 | 1 200 | |
| Other expenses | 9 000 | 450 | 350 | 400 | |
| **Total expenses** | 10 800 | 2 350 | 2 550 | 2 800 | Add all expenses together |
| **Net cash flow** | (6 800) | 2 150 | 2 950 | 3 700 | Total income – total expenses |
| Opening balance bought forward | 0 | (6 800) | (4 650) | (1 700) | The previous months closing balance |
| Closing balance carried forward | (6 800) | (4 650) | (1 700) | 2 000 | Opening balance + net cashflow |

( ) are used to show that a number is negative.

## Solutions to cash flow problems
**Reschedule payments** i.e. slow down the flow of money going out of the business
- Negotiate credit terms with suppliers e.g. buy now pay in 30 days
- May lose discounts for early payment

**Overdrafts**
- Short term source of finance that can be used to provide cash
  - Can be prearranged with the bank
  - May increase costs and future outflows in interest payments

**Reduce the amount of money flowing out**
- Can you reduce costs e.g. find a cheaper supplier
- Might have a negative effect on quality

### Increase the amount of money flowing in
- Take out a loan or attract more customers
- Either option will incur additional costs e.g. interest payments on a loan or need to advertise to attract more customers

### Find new sources of finance
- Bring new funds into the business. For example, from a bank loan or investors e.g. a new share issue

### Reschedule income i.e. speed up the flow of money coming into the business
- Get customers to pay quicker or possibly in advance e.g. pay a deposit
- May lose customers if a competitor is offering credit

*MarketInvoice was set up to help small businesses access cash from unpaid invoices. The invoices are auctioned, e-Bay style, to larger financial institutions. This provides cash flow to the small business and allows the financial institutions to use their specialist skills to chase up the invoice. Although the small business will not get the full amount of the invoice they will have cash flow to help to pay for the day to day running of the business e.g. wages.*

### Cash and profit are different
**Profit** exists in financial records when total revenue is greater than total costs. **Cash** is the physical existence of money within the business. Profitable businesses can fail because of a lack of cash. Reasons why cash and profit might be different include:
- Credit sales
- Bad debts
- Heavy stock holdings
- Investment in fixed assets
- Seasonality
- Repayment of loans

# Test Yourself

## 1.3.3 Cash and cash flow

1. What is cash flow?
2. State two consequences of cash flow problems.
3. Briefly explain one effect of positive cash flow.

|  | Month 1 £ | Month 2 £ | Month 3 £ |
|---|---|---|---|
| Cash inflows from sales | 600 | 1800 | 2600 |
| **Expenses** | | | |
| Rent | 400 | 400 | 400 |
| Materials | 200 | | 1300 |
| Other expenses | 1900 | 1200 | 1500 |
| Total expenses | | 2400 | 3200 |
| Net cash flow | (1900) | (600) | |
| Opening balance | 3000 | | 500 |
| Closing balance | 1100 | 500 | |

4. Calculate the total expenses in month 1.
5. Calculate the materials in month 2.
6. Calculate the opening balance in month 2.
7. Calculate the net cash flow in month 3.
8. Calculate the closing balance in month 3.
9. State two solutions to cash flow problems.
10. Briefly explain the difference between cash and profit.

# 1.3.4 Sources of business finance

**What you need to learn**
- Sources of finance for a start-up or established small business:
  - short-term sources: overdraft and trade credit
  - long-term sources: personal savings, venture capital, share capital, loans, retained profit and crowd funding

Short-term sources of business finance are those that are likely to be used for up to a period of one year. These will include:

### Overdraft
The ability to withdraw more money from a bank current account than you actually have.
Interest rates are often very high.

| Advantages | Disadvantages |
| --- | --- |
| Only borrowed when required, allowing flexibility. | The bank can call it in at any time. |
| Only pay for the money borrowed. | Only available from a current bank account. |
| Relatively quick and easy to arrange. | Interest payments tend to be variable, therefore making it more difficult to budget. |
| No charges for paying off the overdraft. | Banks may secure the overdraft against the business' assets. |

### Trade credit
Goods or services are received now but paid for at a later date.
A supplier will normally allow other businesses a set amount of time e.g. 28 days before payment is required.
This can be a lifeline when a business has cash flow problems.

| Advantages | Disadvantages |
| --- | --- |
| Receive the products now but don't need to pay until a later date. | May lose out on discounts available for cash or early payments. |
| Helps resolve short-term cash flow issues. | Dependent upon a good relationship with suppliers. |

Long-term sources of business finance are those that are likely to be used for a period of more than one year. These will include:

### Personal savings
When an entrepreneur invests their own money in a business e.g. from their own savings.
Owner's capital is how much the owner has invested in the business.

| Advantages | Disadvantages |
|---|---|
| There is no need to pay interest or even repay finance. | Amount available may be limited. |
| Retention of ownership by the individual. | Puts stress on the day to day finance of the individual e.g. still have to pay mortgage or monthly bills. |

### Venture capital
Investment from an established business into another business in return for a percentage equity in the business. Also known as private equity finance.

| Advantages | Disadvantages |
|---|---|
| Potential for large sums of money for investment. | A long and complex process |
| Expertise to help the business. | Expert financial projections are likely to be required. |
| Makes it easier to attract other sources of finance. | Risk of conflict or perceived interference. |
| Provides the required capital for expansion. | Initially expensive for the business e.g. legal and accounting fees. |
| | Partial loss of ownership. |

## Share capital

Shares represent ownership of a company. If you hold one share worth £1 in a multi-billion £ company then you are a part owner.

Shareholders will receive a dividend (a share of the profits) and be given a voting right.

The amount of dividend payable will vary year on year and depend upon profit levels and company objectives.

Appropriate source for raising large amounts of finance, but only an option for companies.

| Advantages | Disadvantages |
| --- | --- |
| No need to repay. | Shareholders will expect to be paid dividends from profits, hence reducing retained profit available to fund expansion. |
| Does not incur interest payments. | |
| Can raise the profile of the company, as seen as a sign of confidence. | The original owners may see a loss of control. |
| | If the new shares are not purchased this could lead to bad publicity. |

## Loans

A set amount of money borrowed from the bank, normally for a specific purpose, to be paid back over a period of time, with a fixed interest rate e.g. 5 years at 6% of the initial sum per annum. Interest has to be paid on the amount borrowed.

Banks may require security on the loan, known as collateral. This can be an asset of the business owner or the company e.g. house, factory.

A mortgage is a long term loan secured against an asset, normally a building.

| Advantages | Disadvantages |
| --- | --- |
| Relatively quick and easy to secure, especially for established businesses with assets. | Interest must be paid regardless of profit levels. |
| Fixed interest rates allowing businesses to budget more easily. | A business normally provides security against its assets. |
| Improved cash flow. | Often more expensive than other forms of finance. |
| The borrower retains ownership of the company. | A business can be charged for early payment. |

## Retained profit

Profit kept within the business from profit after tax to help finance future activity.

Profit will either be retained or distributed as dividends.

A business with an objective of growth is likely to want to maximise retained profit without alienating shareholders.

| Advantages | Disadvantages |
|---|---|
| Internal, therefore no need to repay. | May be limited funds available. |
| Instantly available. | Shareholders may prefer to see short term returns on their investments. |
| Does not incur additional costs such as interest payments. | Not an option for a start-up business. |
| Control is not lost. | |

## Crowd funding

Raising finance from a large number of people each investing different, often small, amounts of money. The investor is only tied into their promised contribution if the total amount is raised.

| Advantages | Disadvantages |
|---|---|
| The business can use the internet to explain how much money is required, how it will be used and the exit strategy stating predicted return on the investment. | Often fail to raise the finance required. |
| Low cost and quick way of raising finance. | Allows competitors to see ideas and valuable information about the business. |
| A form of marketing as people will see the business profile whether they invest or not. | |

# Test Yourself

## 1.3.4 Sources of business finance

1. What are short-term sources of finance?

2. What are long-term sources of finance?

3. Explain one advantage and one disadvantage of using an overdraft as a source of finance.

4. Explain one advantage and one disadvantage of using trade credit as a source of finance.

5. Explain one advantage and one disadvantage of using personal savings as a source of finance.

6. Explain one advantage and one disadvantage of using venture capital as a source of finance.

7. Explain one advantage and one disadvantage of using share capital as a source of finance.

8. Explain one advantage and one disadvantage of using a loan as a source of finance.

9. Explain one advantage and one disadvantage of using retained profit as a source of finance.

10. Explain one advantage and one disadvantage of using crowd funding as a source of finance.

## 1.4.1 The options for start-up and small businesses

**What you need to learn**
- The concept of limited liability:
  - limited and unlimited liability
  - the implications for the business (s) of limited and unlimited liability
- The types of business ownership for start-ups:
  - sole trader, partnership, private limited company
  - the advantages and disadvantages of each type of business ownership
- The option of starting up and running a franchise operation:
  - the advantages and disadvantages of franchising

**Legal structure** refers to the **ownership** of a business.

These two terms are key to understanding legal structure:
**Unlimited liability** means that the owner(s) is personally responsible for all of the debts of the business. This acts as a safeguard against overspending but could mean that the owner loses their **personal assets.**
**Limited liability** means that the owner(s) debts are limited to the amount invested in the firm. This allows owners to invest without fear of losing their **personal assets**.

There are implications to a business of having limited or unlimited liability. These include:

- the ease with which finance can be raised
- attitudes to risk
- relationships with suppliers e.g. ability to buy goods now but pay at a later date

## Sole traders

A sole trader is an individual who owns and runs their own business.
- The simplest form of business • A sole trader has unlimited liability
- They could lose their home and all of their assets to pay off any debts

| Sole trader - Advantages | Sole trader - Disadvantages |
|---|---|
| Cheap and easy to set up | Unlimited liability |
| Keep all the profits for themselves | Hard work |
| Accounts are private – cannot be seen by competitors | Limited finance available |
| Own boss making all the decisions | The owner has to do everything or 'buy in' expertise |

## Partnerships

A partnership is where two or more people run the business.
- Each partner is equally responsible for the debts of the business
- Each partner will take a share of the profits
- Each partner usually shares in the decision making
- 'Sleeping' partners invest in, but do not run, the business
- Setting up a business involves writing a **"deed of partnership"**

| Partnership - Advantages | Partnership - Disadvantages |
|---|---|
| Risks and responsibilities shared | Unlimited liability |
| Different skills and expertise | Disagreements can occur between partners |
| Shared finance – each partner invests making it easier to raise finance | If a partner dies, resigns or goes bankrupt the partnership is dissolved i.e. it stops existing |
| More input and ideas | Each partner can make legally binding decisions - trust |

## Private limited company
A private limited company is owned by shareholders.
- Ltd. after the company name
- The shareholders are often family members
- Private limited companies exist in their own right i.e. the owners and the company are separate legal entities
- The company's finances are separate from the owner's personal finances

## Shareholders
- Invest money to buy part of (a share in) the business
- They are part owners and receive a share of the profit in the form of **dividends**
- They have limited liability, can only lose the money that they have invested
- Have a say in the running of the business – **a voting right**

| Private limited company - Advantages | Private limited company - Disadvantages |
|---|---|
| Limited liability | More complex to set up – paperwork & registration |
| Easier to raise finance – sell shares | Accounts are available for anyone to see |
| More expertise available | Possible loss of control |
| Separate legal entity | Limited liability may be seen as a risk by suppliers and banks |
| Continues to exist even when shareholders change | |

Private limited companies must be registered (**Incorporated**). They must send to **Companies House**:
- A Memorandum of Association
    - name, registered office and what the company will do
- Articles of Association
    - the rules of running the company
- An annual set of accounts
    - that can be requested by anyone, including the competitors!

*The Cambridge Satchel Company was set up by Julie Deane and her mother Freda Thomas in 2008. The company produces colourful leather satchels that might look at home in a Harry Potter movie. As with many family run businesses it has private limited company status. This has made it easier for the business to finance expansion. In 2008 it was producing 3 handmade satchels a week. By 2012 turnover had reached £10 million and the company had opened its first store in Covent Garden.*

## Franchising

A franchise is when one business (the franchisor) gives another person or business (the franchisee) the right to trade using its name and to sell its products or provide its services.

The franchisee normally pays a licence fee and a percentage of profit to the franchisor.

| Franchising - Advantages | Franchising - Disadvantages |
| --- | --- |
| Established brand name | Normally requires an initial cost to obtain the franchise and ongoing costs to retain it |
| Help and advice from the franchisor in a number of areas such as location and recruitment | Often requires raw materials to be bought from the franchisee |
| Opportunities available in a number of locations | Strict rules apply as to how the franchisee can operate |

## Test Yourself

### 1.3.5 The options for start-up and small businesses

1. What is meant by limited and unlimited liability?

2. State and explain two features of a sole trader.

3. Explain one advantage and one disadvantage of a sole trader.

4. State and explain two features of a partnership.

5. Explain one advantage and one disadvantage of a partnership.

6. State and explain two features of a private limited company.

7. Explain one advantage and one disadvantage of a private limited company.

8. Explain one reason why individuals would choose to be a private limited company rather than a partnership.

9. State and explain two features of a franchise.

10. Explain one advantage and one disadvantage of being a franchisee.

## 1.4.2 Business location

> **What you need to learn**
> - Factors influencing business location:
>   - proximity to: market, labour, materials and competitors
>   - nature of the business activity
>   - the impact of the internet on location decisions: e-commerce and/or fixed premises

**Best location** is the business location that provides the maximum benefits to a business through the combination of **quantitative** and **qualitative** factors.

Many, if not all, growing businesses will have **maximising profit** as one of their main objectives. This helps keep shareholders happy. Remember **profit = revenues - costs**. Therefore, when choosing the best location a business will want to achieve 2 things:
- Minimised costs
- Increased revenue

There are number of key factors influencing the location decision of a business.

### 1. Proximity to the market
Businesses will consider how close they want to be to their customers.
- A location that has a large footfall helps to attract passing trade
- Bulk gaining firms will want to be close to customers to reduce costs i.e. the end product is a lot bigger than the raw materials
- Convenient for the customer

## 2. Proximity to labour
Labour refers to whether there are enough workers, with the right skills, who are willing to work for the business in any given location.
- Need for specialist skills or knowledge
- Wages demanded – in an area of high unemployment wages may be lower, reducing costs

**What firms are located close to where you live?**
**Why do you think they chose to locate there?**

## 3. Proximity to materials
**Raw materials** are the physical inputs that go into producing a good or providing a service.
- Some firms have no choice e.g. mining or fishing
- Bulk reducing firms will want to be close to raw materials to reduce costs i.e. the end product is a lot smaller than the raw materials
- Ability to produce quality raw materials e.g. good land for farming or sunshine for growing crops

*"In Britain today - two out of three apples harvested are of the Cox variety and are homegrown in the countryside of Kent, Sussex, Suffolk, East Anglia and the West Midlands."*
Source: http://www.copellafruitjuices.co.uk

**Why is Copella located in Suffolk?**

## 4. Proximity to competitors
Other businesses in an area may be good if they attract customers to the area or provide support services. Equally, it can be bad if it means each business only attracts a few customers.
- High levels of competition may mean it is hard to gain a foothold in the market
- Sometimes competition is good because customers are attracted to an area where they have lots of choice e.g. a shopping centre
- Other businesses may offer services to support the business e.g. banks, office cleaning and distribution

## 5. Nature of the business activity
A start-up business will have limited finance so will have to consider carefully the cost of different locations.
- Popular/busy areas tend to be a lot more expensive e.g. city and town centres and new shopping arcades compared to side streets or out of town locations
- Wage rates vary in different parts of the country depending upon the availability of workers and the cost of living

*In 2013 a new £350 million retail and leisure complex was opened in Leeds. Transport to Leeds is excellent and the train station is less than 100 metres away. The new development, Trinity Leeds, has lured shoppers away from other areas such as Manchester's Trafford Centre and Sheffield's Meadowhall. Alongside 120 shops one of the new residents was the Everyman Cinema. This was the first Everyman cinema outside of London. With the biggest financial and legal sector outside of London Everyman believed there was plenty of demand for a high quality cinema in Leeds. Although costs were high there was a lack of competition in Leeds city centre, Vue Cinema being the only main competitor. Leeds City Council also saw potential in the city, opening a 13 500 seater music venue, the First Direct Arena.*

**What were the main reasons Everyman Cinemas chose to locate in Leeds? Can you list them in order of importance?**

Businesses are not all the same and have varied requirements. These will include:
- Infrastructure required
    - Businesses that deliver goods need a road, rail and air network in order to deliver these quickly and effectively
    - Businesses who have a physical presence will need customers to be able to access them easily
- Pool of skilled workers required
    - Finance/legal sector often locate in large urban centres, especially London, where there are a large number of specialist workers to choose from
    - Certain industries e.g. the shoe industry have developed historically in one area so there is a pool of workers available
- Other factors include:
    - A prestigious address
    - High footfall
    - Costs, including transport, utilities and business rates
- Some businesses may look to locate abroad to benefit from low costs of premises and labour

## 6. The impact of the internet on location decisions: e-commerce and/or fixed premises.
- The Internet has made the world a smaller place to trade
    - Smaller businesses can now target customers on a global basis
- **E-commerce** has seen the rapid expansion of online markets
    - Specialist businesses have created market places for third parties to trade on e.g. Amazon and e-Bay
    - Any business can buy and sell, with easy access to customers and suppliers
- Businesses no longer need **fixed premises**
    - Costs are cheaper for start-up businesses as they do not require offices or 'bricks and mortar' physical stores
    - Often, employees can work from home as most people have the facilities to connect to the Internet

# Test Yourself

**1.4.2 Business location**

1. What is meant by business location?

2. Explain why the proximity to the market is important to a business when choosing location.

3. Explain why the proximity to labour is important to a business when choosing location.

4. Explain why the proximity to materials is important to a business when choosing location.

5. Explain why the proximity to competitors is important to a business when choosing location.

6. State one type of business that may want to locate close to competitors. Justify your answer.

7. Explain one reason why the nature of business activity will impact on the location of a business.

8. What is meant by e-commerce?

9. Explain why e-commerce can impact on the location decisions of a business.

10. Explain why having fixed premises can impact negatively on the costs of a business.

# 1.4.3 The marketing mix

**What you need to learn**
- What the marketing mix is and the importance of each element:
  - price, product, promotion, place

- How the elements of the marketing mix work together:
  - balancing the marketing mix based on the competitive environment
  - the impact of changing consumer needs on the marketing mix
  - the impact of technology on the marketing mix: e-commerce, digital communication

## What is the marketing mix?
- The effective combination of the four key elements of marketing, known as the four Ps
  - Price
  - Product
  - Promotion
  - Place

| Price | Product |
|---|---|
| How much a business will charge for the good being sold or service provided. | The goods and services that a business provides. |
| Businesses use different pricing methods to price their products, taking into account a number of factors such as market research, number of competitors and the state of the economy. | Goods are physical or tangible products. You can touch them e.g. a car or a television. Services are unphysical or intangible. They cannot be touched e.g. financial consultancy or teaching. |//

| Promotion | Place |
|---|---|
| The activities designed to communicate with the market thereby increasing visibility and sales of a product. | The means by which the product will be distributed, where the customer will be able to buy the product. |
| It aims to inform and persuade customers about a product and to create Awareness, Interest, Desire and Action (AIDA). Businesses use different promotional methods to make their products more widely known to other businesses and to the general public e.g. branding, advertising and sponsorship. | This can be physical e.g. a shop, wholesaler or market place, or virtual i.e. a website. The type of product, the reputation and branding of the business, the number of competitors and the type of customer will dictate how far the customer is prepared to travel to purchase the good or service. |

In order to be effective, the 4 elements must complement each other. For example, a designer product will have a high price tag, be available to buy from a prestigious store and be promoted using an appropriate advertisement.

**How the elements of the marketing mix work together**

**1. Balancing the marketing mix based on the competitive environment**

In a market dominated by a few large businesses there is likely to be non-price competition:
- Businesses will compete on the quality of the product
- There will be heavy spending on promotion
- Place will be important as customers will wish to access the product easily, whether physically or online

In a market where there is plenty of competition price will be significant:
- Consumers will be able to shop around, making place important
- Promotion for small businesses will be less expensive, perhaps through local media such as local newspapers
- There will be low barriers to entering the market and businesses will try to differentiate their products, perhaps through the quality of customer service

**2. The impact of changing consumer needs on the marketing mix**

As society changes so do the needs of consumers:
Technological developments lead to new products being created
- Businesses can charge higher prices for the latest technology
- Methods of promotion change as social media develops
- Channels of distribution change and many businesses now have a multi-channel approach i.e. selling products in a variety of different ways such as in store and online

Changes in demographics lead to different target markets
- Mass immigration has led to a cosmopolitan society with different consumer needs, so new products are required. These will be marketed in different ways in order to target these new markets
- As the population ages the 'grey pound', old aged pensioners, also require new products appropriate to their needs

The state of the economy impacts on consumer incomes
- When the economy is in decline there is a greater demand for cheaper products
- When the economy is doing well people have higher disposable incomes and the demand for more expensive products increases

## 3. The impact of technology on the marketing mix: e-commerce, digital communication

E-commerce has transformed the buying habits of consumers
- It is easy for buyers and sellers to come together to exchange goods and services electronically
- New products have been created, such as streaming music and videos
- This has led to different forms of promotion and pricing strategies
- New channels of distribution, such as the use of massive warehouses to deliver goods, have developed around e-commerce

Digital communication has impacted significantly on the marketing mix
- Social media has made it easier for businesses to interact with customers in order to promote their products
- Pricing strategies and promotions can be aimed at the specific customer, as businesses build up a consumer profile using cookies and other market research methods

# Test Yourself

## 1.4.3 The marketing mix

1. What is the marketing mix?

2. What is price?

3. What is product?

4. What is promotion?

5. What is place?

6. Explain the marketing mix of a business you are familiar with.

7. Explain why the marketing mix will be impacted by the degree of competition in the market.

8. Explain why the marketing mix will be impacted by changing needs of consumers.

9. With the use of an example, explain why the marketing mix needs to be integrated.

10. Explain one impact of technology on the marketing mix.

## 1.4.4 Business plans

> **What you need to learn**
> - The role and importance of a business plan:
>   - to identify: the business idea; business aims and objectives; target market (market research); forecast revenue, cost and profit; cash-flow forecast; sources of finance; location; marketing mix
> - The purpose of planning business activity:
>   - the role and importance of a business plan in minimising risk and obtaining finance

### What is a business plan?
"A business plan is a written document that describes a business, its objectives, its strategies, the market it is in and its financial forecasts."
www.businesslink.gov.uk

### What is the **purpose of business planning**?
A business plan is used both internally, for use by the firm's management, and externally, by banks and external investors.

A business plan is important in setting up a new business. It helps the entrepreneur consider, in detail, all of the aspects of the business. This provides a guide to follow to help ensure all necessary steps are completed and therefore, provides a sense of direction.

The role and importance of a business plan in order to identify:
**Business idea**
- This provides a guide to follow to help ensure all necessary steps are completed to bring this idea to reality
- Provides a sense of direction

**Business aims and objectives**
- These should be SMART to allow the business to measure progress and performance
- Provides motivation

## Target market (market research)
- Provides a focus on the market research that will need to be undertaken in order to develop an understanding of the market

## Forecast revenue, cost and profit; cash flow forecast, sources of finance
- The business plan helps the entrepreneur identify financial factors that are fundamental to the business' success and in gaining finance, particularly from banks
- It will identify where sources of funding will come from and how many products will need to be sold to break-even
- Budgets can be drawn up to identify forecast revenues, expenditure and profits

## Location
- Where the business will locate and why, including proximity to market, suppliers and employees as well as the infrastructure in the surrounding area

## Marketing mix
- How the integrated mix will work in achieving success for the business

Business planning **minimises risk** and gives a structure to the activities of the business
- helps to focus on the mission and clarifies objectives
- provides a template to measure progress and performance
- encourages a logical approach, outlining what needs to be done

A business plan is essential to **obtaining finance** from external investors, including the bank
- finance providers will want a detailed breakdown of how the business is going to be successful and how they will get a return on their funding

## The main sections within a business start-up plan

| Section details | Section name |
|---|---|
| Goods or services to be provided<br>Name • Legal structure<br>Entrepreneur(s) – skills and experience | Description of the business |
| The short, medium and long term goals<br>How will it measure success? | Aims and objectives |
| Summary of market research carried out<br>Key findings e.g. customer data, customers' opinions<br>Analysis of competition | Research results |
| Target market – what are the characteristics of the customer<br>The marketing mix – product, place, price and promotion<br>Future plans e.g. new products | Marketing |
| Number and type of workers to be employed<br>Skills of management and workforce | HRM |
| Location • Production process<br>Suppliers • Targets for output<br>Actions for ensuring quality and meeting customer needs | Operations |
| Sources of finance • Forecast costs and revenues<br>Forecast profit (or loss) over several years<br>Cash flow statement | Financial information |

**Advice from the Prince's Trust** *"The best business plans aren't long and complex; they explain only the most important information – what you want to achieve, how you will get there and the things you need to do along the way. It's best to tackle a business plan in small chunks."*

## Test Yourself

### 1.4.4 Business plans

1. What is a business plan?

2. Explain two reasons why businesses create business plans.

3. Explain the main sections of a business plan.

4. Explain two benefits of business planning.

5. Explain two drawbacks of business planning.

6. Explain why a business plan will help to identify the business idea.

7. Explain why a business plan will help to identify the target market.

8. Explain why a business plan will help to identify business aims and objectives.

9. Explain why a business plan will help to identify forecast revenue, cost and profit.

10. Explain why a business plan will help to identify a suitable location for a business.

## 1.5.1 Business stakeholders

**What you need to learn**
- Who business stakeholders are and their different objectives:
  - shareholders (owners), employees, customers, managers, suppliers, local community, pressure groups, the government
- Stakeholders and businesses:
  - how stakeholders are affected by business activity
  - how stakeholders impact business activity
  - possible conflicts between stakeholder groups

**Stakeholders** are anyone with an interest in the activities of a business. They can influence the business' objectives. Who are the stakeholders in a business?

- **Internal** – people or groups inside the business
  - Owners/shareholders • Employees
- **External** – people or groups outside the business
  - Customers • Local community • Suppliers • Banks • Government

| Stakeholder | Main objectives |
| --- | --- |
| Shareholders | A company will want high dividend payments for shareholders. A dividend is a share of the profit paid to shareholders as a reward for their investment. |
| | Sole traders and partnerships will want the business to be profitable in order for them to achieve financial rewards. |
| | A not-for-profit business will want a large surplus of revenue over costs to support the cause. |
| | Other objectives may include a good reputation and an opportunity to expand. |
| Employees | A key objective will be to maximise pay. |
| | Employees will also want to be paid on time, have good working conditions, be treated fairly, opportunities for promotion, health and safety needs met and provided with training. |
| Customers | Customers will want their needs to be met. This includes good quality goods and services, high levels of satisfaction, reliability, pleasant staff, convenience, value for money, range of facilities e.g. plenty of car parking and clear and accurate information. |

| Stakeholder | Main objectives |
|---|---|
| Suppliers | Suppliers will want to be treated fairly. This will include to be paid on time, good communications, fair pay for goods and services provided, testimonials and regular demand. |
| Managers | As senior members of the organisation these will seek to influence decision making. Their effectiveness is reflected by the success of the business. In return it is expected that they will receive good rates of pay and employment contracts. |
| Local community | Local communities will want the business to minimise the environmental impact. This will include maximising the positive impacts e.g. creating jobs and supporting local causes and minimising the negative impacts e.g. congestion and pollution. |
| Pressure groups | These seek to further specific causes. They have a range of objectives and will try to influence decision making by businesses and individuals e.g. Government officials such as MPs. Examples include trade unions, Greenpeace and Amnesty International. |
| The government | This will include both central Government (from Westminster) and local councils. They make decisions that affect all businesses and individuals in an attempt to enact policies. These will include government spending plans, taxation and creating legislation. |

**What are your objectives as a customer and a member of the local community?**

Stakeholders are affected by business activity on a daily basis, both positively and negatively

- A business that has an objective of growth is likely to create new jobs, benefiting employees, government and the local community. Management might receive higher pay as the business grows in size and suppliers will get more custom. Alternatively, the business might look to downsize, impacting negatively on jobs
- A business will consider which stakeholders are the most influential and prioritise their wants. In doing this it will consider both the level of power and the level of interest they have

*Which? is a consumer watchdog that carries out research and reports its findings to promote informed consumer choice. It gains high levels of media interest. On Easter Sunday 2018 it reported that up to a third of the weight of an Easter Egg can be made up of packaging. The worst offender was Thorntons with 36% of its Classic Large Egg being made up of cardboard and plastic. Thornton's defended its actions saying that this was to maintain freshness.*

Businesses may face conflict between stakeholders. This occurs when one stakeholder achieves its objective but, in doing this, has a negative impact on another stakeholder.

| | Examples of stakeholder conflict | |
|---|---|---|
| Owners – high dividends | Conflict may arise as high dividends are likely to come from the ability of the business to maximise profit. Pay is a cost to a business. If employees maximise pay this is likely to lead to a fall in profits and therefore lower dividends. | Employees – maximise pay |
| Suppliers – fair pay for goods and services | Conflict may arise as, if the business pays a fair rate to suppliers, this will increase its costs. These increased costs may be passed on to the customer in the form of higher prices. | Customers – low prices |

# Test Yourself

## 1.5.1 Business stakeholders

1. What is a stakeholder?

2. State five main stakeholders of a business.

3. What is a stakeholder's objective?

4. For each stakeholder state and explain one objective.

5. State two ways that stakeholders can influence business.

6. What is a stakeholder conflict?

7. Explain why conflict may arise between employees and owners.

8. Explain one other example of stakeholder conflict.

9. Explain why employees and consumers might agree on decisions made by management.

10. Explain why shareholders are often seen as the most important stakeholder in a business.

## 1.5.2 Technology and business

**What you need to learn**
- Different types of technology used by business:
  - e-commerce
  - social media
  - digital communication
  - payment systems

- How technology influences business activity in terms of:
  - sales
  - costs
  - marketing mix

**Technology** is the use of scientific advancements. It has had a massive impact not only on the types of goods and services that we buy but also on how and where we buy them, how they are produced and how we pay for them. It has created opportunities e.g. access to new markets and threats e.g. new substitute products for businesses.

Technology impacts on all four of the functional areas of a business:
- Business operations
  - use of machinery to produce goods, automated stock control systems, computer aided design, customer service via online chatrooms
- Human resources
  - ability to work from home, different skills required, communication methods e.g. Skype
- Marketing
  - use of digital communications e.g. social media, internet sales, direct marketing via email, use of websites for promotional purposes
- Finance
  - online payments to suppliers and from customers, online monitoring of bank balances and payments, ability to search for cheaper supplies

E-commerce is when buyers and sellers come together to trade in a virtual location i.e. over the internet. This has had a significant impact on businesses including:
- The ease with which businesses can access wider markets e.g. sell abroad
- The ability to trade 24/7
- Development of new services e.g. click and collect or online ordering
- Offers a cheaper alternative to new start-up businesses
- Greater convenience to customers e.g. you can now book your hair appointment or a table at a restaurant online
- The need to develop secure payment systems to give consumers confidence

| E-commerce | | | |
|---|---|---|---|
| Business operations | Human resources | Marketing | Finance |
| Warehouse logistics to meet demand and delivery expectations of customers. May need to hold large amounts of stock. | Change of job roles e.g. check out operator to online picker. Loss of jobs e.g. due to closure of high street stores. | Has helped change place in the marketing mix. Use of social media, blogs and internet for promotional activity. Ease of price comparisons. | Secure online payment methods. Ability to search for cheaper suppliers to reduce costs. |

**Social media** is the use of the internet to allow individuals and organisations to participate in social networking. This allows businesses to gain an insight into customer needs and wants. It can be used as a means to promote the business, creating brand awareness, loyalty and repeat custom. It allows for rapid sharing of information and is a cheap and easy form of promotion for the business.

Digital communication is the transfer of data that has been stored or processed by technology. Examples of digital communication include the use of:
- Computers
- Internet
- Cell phones
- Smart TVs
- Tablets

This has changed the way that businesses communicate with stakeholders.

| Stakeholder | Example of digital communication |
|---|---|
| Customers | Businesses now increasingly use social media to communicate with customers. This allows the business to keep followers informed of updates and special offers. It also encourages two way communication with customers, allowing for feedback and to share the business' communication with its own network of people. This may include Twitter, Facebook and Instagram. |
| Employees | Employers can keep in touch with employees and keep them informed using computers and a business network. This could include e-bulletins, e-mails and video conferencing. This reduces the amount of paper communications and reduces costs as face to face meetings are more expensive. This could include the use of an intranet, video conferencing and Skype. Employees may also use tablets to communicate with each other e.g. a waiter sending an order to the kitchen or shop assistant to the store room. |
| Suppliers | Computers have enabled businesses to automate stock control and reordering systems. This has made communication with suppliers much easier. When stock reaches a certain level, an electronic message is automatically sent to a supplier to place an order. |

| Stakeholder | Example of digital communication |
|---|---|
| Owners | Updates and reports such as the year-end Chairperson's statement are now more likely to be sent electronically than via post. |
| Community | Members of the community can be updated with information about events, job opportunities and achievements via social media. This could include blogs, Twitter feeds and e-newsletters. |
| Government | Important actions such as paying VAT and corporation tax bills can now be completed quickly online. This increases convenience for both the business and the Government. |

*High Street stores are facing increasingly difficult market conditions. One major threat is the continued growth of online retailer Amazon. In an attempt to entice customers back into stores retailers are turning to technology to enhance the shoppers' experience. One initiative, by Nike, involves integrating the customer into interactive videos. Whilst trying on their new trainers the customer can view themselves on large screens jumping over buildings or dancing with pandas.*

**Online payment systems** allow for individuals and businesses to easily pay for goods and services. This can be through both e-commerce and m-commerce. This allows for quick and easy business to business (B2B) transactions with suppliers, banks, employment agencies, service providers e.g. cleaning contractors and professional services e.g. accountants. It also allows for quick and effective payment for business to consumer (B2C) transactions, meaning greater convenience and higher sales.

Technology influences business activity in terms of:

**Sales**
- Big data has allowed businesses to analyse massive amounts of customer data, giving insight into consumer behaviour and buying habits
    - This allows businesses to specifically target consumers
- Social media has meant that products are sold through building strong relationships with customers
    - This can require a dedicated sales and marketing team, but is also accessible to any size business
- Sales Force Automation (SFA) systematises tasks, allowing computers to undertake repetitive and boring everyday jobs
    - This frees up the sales team or entrepreneur, meaning that they can spend time on generating sales that create added value
- Cloud technology allowing the sales force to access business and customer data instantly
    - This allows the sales force to access information about the products and the customers
- E-commerce and m-commerce, making it quick and easy to sell products

**Costs**
- Communication costs have fallen significantly
    - The use of e-mail to contact customers and websites to promote the full range of products has reduced spending on areas such as postal and catalogue costs
- Small businesses can market their products on a low budget through websites
- Paperwork can be reduced significantly by keeping digital records
- Video conferencing and skype can reduce meeting costs, with no travelling expenses or the need to hire meeting rooms
- Cloud technology allows for easy storage of, and easy access to, information

## Marketing mix

- Price
    - As technology lowers the costs of delivering products it means that businesses can lower price if appropriate
    - Customers have a greater choice of products, meaning that they can shop around for lower prices
- Product
    - New product development is easier as businesses can use new processes such as 3D printing or streaming products such as music and films
- Promotion
    - The use of cookies allows businesses to target specific customers
    - Social media used to promote brand awareness
- Place
    - Websites allowing for e-commerce
    - M-commerce allowing customers to order products anywhere, at any time

Josh March and Dan Lester worked for iPlatform where they developed social applications for Facebook. They believed that businesses faced problems in developing their use of social media through websites such as Facebook and Twitter. Their market research suggested only 35% of questions to big businesses on social media received a response. This led to negative feedback regarding the brand. Josh and Dan realised that nearly all of the big businesses that they looked at were concerned about developing secure and meaningful conversations through social media sites. This applied both externally, with customers, and internally, with staff. They launched Conversocial, a new business dedicated to helping businesses get the most out of social networks. This was about more than just marketing. Through their market research they had realised that social networks had a range of uses e.g. developing customer service. This has led to them developing specialist software for a range of big names such as Tesco, the Carphone Warehouse and Groupon. A single employee can respond to over 1000 Facebook and Twitter comments in an hour by using Conversocial software.

# Test Yourself

## 1.5.2 Technology and business

1. What is technology?

2. State one way in which technology influences business operations.

3. State one way in which technology influences marketing.

4. State one way in which technology influences finance.

5. State one way in which technology influences human resources.

6. What is e-commerce?

7. Explain how e-commerce can help businesses access wider markets.

8. State, with examples, two types of digital technology.

9. Explain how digital technology has changed the way a business communicates with two different stakeholder groups.

10. Explain one way in which technology can impact on the marketing mix of a business.

## 1.5.3 Legislation and business

**What you need to learn**
- The purpose of legislation:
  - principles of consumer law: quality and consumer rights
  - principles of employment law: recruitment, pay, discrimination and health and safety
- The impact of legislation on businesses:
  - cost
  - consequences of meeting and not meeting these obligations

**Legislation** is law passed, mainly through Acts of Parliament. There are a number of laws that are designed to protect the rights of the consumers and the workforce.

These laws **impact** on a business because:
- Increased costs:
  - Wage costs may be higher
  - Additional expenses e.g. health and safety equipment and training
  - Ensuring premises are accessible to all e.g. lifts and ramps if necessary
- Could be taken to court if the laws are ignored and legal action taken:
  - Fined
  - Prosecuted including possible imprisonment
  - Closed down
- The reputation of the business may suffer if the business fails to follow the laws:
  - Bad publicity
  - Loss of customers

However they could help motivate workers who feel they are fairly treated and safe.

The benefits of providing a safe working environment include:
- Could help motivate workers who feel they are fairly treated and safe
- Easier to recruit and retain workers
- Avoid fines and negative publicity
- No loss of time whilst issues are resolved or accidents dealt with

**Employment laws**

These are laws that attempt to protect all employees by giving them certain entitlements (rights).
- Terms and conditions of employment should be laid out in a contract of employment e.g. holiday entitlement, working hours and disciplinary procedures
- Rights of employees in terms of maternity and paternity leave
- Protecting an employee against unfair dismissal

Employment laws include:
- National minimum wage /living wage
- The Equality Act (2010)
- Health and Safety Act (1974)

In 2015 Deputy Prime Minister Nick Clegg introduced changes to flexible working hours. Changes meant that employees are able to work from home and work flexible hours rather than the standard 9 to 5. New mums are able to share maternity leave with their partners – meaning that they can share 50 weeks off work between them. This will encourage more women into the workplace. Changes have been welcomed by unions. Some small business owners have criticised the changes saying that it has made it impossible to coordinate employees in the workplace and costs have risen.

## National minimum wage/living wage

The National Minimum Wage Act 1998 states that businesses must pay at least a minimum wage per hour to all employees. The amount is based upon the age of the employee.

In April 2016 the Government introduced the National Living Wage. From April 2019 this rate was £8.21 per hour for people aged 25 and over. The amount is reviewed, and amended, annually by the low pay commission. Check out what the current rate is at https://www.gov.uk/national-minimum-wage-rates .

As pay for people over 25 is greater than that for those under 25 there might be the temptation for some employers to hire younger workers. An exception is that if a worker is a family member or lives in the family home of the employer then the employer does not have to pay the minimum/living wage. Businesses found guilty of not paying the minimum/living wage can be fined 200% of the wage owed, up to a maximum of £20 000.

The **Living Wage** was set up independently by the Living Wage Foundation. This is a voluntary scheme, mainly impacting on London. Businesses pay a wage that is based on the cost of living.

## The Equality Act 2010

The **Equality Act 2010** replaced previous anti-discrimination laws with a single Act. By bringing together over 116 different laws it makes it easier for the law to be understood and carried out. This law attempts to stop workers from being treated differently i.e. discriminated against.

This will impact significantly on employers who are undertaking **unlawful discrimination** if they treat a job applicant or employee differently because of a **protected characteristic**. These include:

- Age, disability, gender reassignment, marriage and civil partnership, pregnancy and maternity, race, religion or belief, sex, sexual orientation

Employers must ensure that they abide by the law. Otherwise, severe penalties can be applied as well as the impact on the reputation of the business. This will require employee training to educate workers regarding the law and to overcome prejudice that might impact on the recruitment process and occur within the business on a daily basis.

# Health and safety law – The Health and Safety at Work Act 1974

## Health and safety

These laws look after the rights of the workforce in terms of their **wellbeing** in the workplace.

- A business has to provide the correct training to employees to ensure the job can be carried out safely
- Provide all necessary safety equipment and where appropriate safety clothing e.g. helmets or steel toe capped boots
- Responsible for ensuring standards are maintained by all employees
- Premises meet minimum standards e.g. toilets and washing facilities
- The work environment is safe e.g. fire exits are kept clear, warnings given near hazardous machines or chemicals and slippery services are identified

## Consumer law

Consumer legislation is designed to protect the consumer from being exploited by businesses. The **Trades Description Act** was originally passed in 1968 and is updated on a regular basis. Its purpose was to ensure that goods and services were sold as described. It is an offence to falsely describe a product. This means that retailers are not allowed to mislead consumers regarding the quality of a product.

Consumer law looks to maintain **quality** defined as what a 'reasonable person' would find acceptable. The product should be fit for purpose, safe and not faulty.

**Consumer rights** are protected by law. These rights include the selling of faulty and counterfeit goods, poor service, rogue traders and issues with contracts and builders.

## Test Yourself

### 1.5.3 Legislation and business

1. What is legislation?

2. Explain how legislation can impact on the costs of a business.

3. State two other impacts of legislation on a business.

4. Explain one reason why the reputation of a business might suffer if it fails to follow legal requirements.

5. What is consumer law?

6. Explain one positive and one negative effect of consumer law on a business.

7. State two areas of employment law.

8. Explain one positive and one negative effect of employment law on a business.

9. What is health and safety law?

10. Explain one positive and one negative effect of health and safety law on a business.

## 1.5.4 The economy and business

**What you need to learn**
- The impact of the economic climate on businesses:
  - unemployment, changing levels of consumer income, inflation, changes in interest rates, government taxation, changes in exchange rates

The **economic climate** is the general state of the economy in a country, or globally, at a given point in time.

Businesses are affected by the economic climate as this affects the costs of the factors of production and consumers' willingness and ability to spend.

### Unemployment
Employment is the number of people who are actively engaged in work. Unemployment is the number of people looking for work but who cannot find a job at a point in time. The reward for labour is a wage or salary.

### Changing levels of consumer income
If the level of employment is high then this indicates a good economic climate. People who are employed will be receiving a wage which will increase demand in the economy. This may mean that prices start to rise as more people are willing and able to buy goods and services. Businesses may see this as an opportunity to invest in order to expand as demand continues to increase. Businesses may also consider the range of products that they offer.

### Changes in interest rates
**Interest rates** are the price of money i.e. the cost of borrowing or the reward for saving.

If a business borrows money from the bank to finance its activities, then it is sensitive to changes in interest rates. A business may have an overdraft or a bank loan which the bank will charge interest on.

- A bank loan is a set amount of money borrowed from the bank to be paid back over a period of time. Interest has to be paid on the amount borrowed
- An overdraft is the ability to withdraw more money from a bank account than you actually have. Interest rates are often very high

If interest rates go up then the bank would charge more for its overdraft and loan repayments. This is an increase in the costs of a business. Faced with increasing costs businesses will have a number of options:

- Increase the price charged to the consumer
- Accept lower profit margins
- Reduce investments to avoid future loans
- Look to cut costs elsewhere

Fluctuating interest rates affect both consumer and business spending.

### Consumer spending

Impacts on the cost of mortgage or loan repayments and therefore the amount of discretionary income consumers have to spend on other goods and services. For example, if interest rates go up a consumer will see their mortgage repayments go up and may have to look to reduce spending on food or clothes to compensate for this.

Affects how expensive it is to buy on credit e.g. using a credit card or finance agreement. This will influence consumers' decisions on whether to spend on credit. This may particularly affect large items of expenditure such as a car or household appliance.

Saving becomes more or less attractive meaning that customers will be influenced on whether to spend or save any spare income. For example, if interest rates are high this may encourage customers to save rather than spend as the reward is greater.

### Business spending

Higher rates of interest will make it more expensive for businesses to borrow money, therefore they are less likely to invest in new machinery, premises or product development. However, if interest rates are low and businesses expect this to continue they will be more willing to invest.

Interest rates are a cost to a business. Therefore, if higher, this represents higher costs and lower levels of profit for future spending.

Businesses understand that interest rates will affect consumer spending which in turn will affect its spending. For example, if a business expects to see a fall in demand as a result of rising interest rates it may look to reduce spending on stock or increase spending on promotional activities.

## Government taxation

Taxation is the process of imposing charges on business and individuals by the government. For example businesses are charged corporation tax on profits. Consumers are charged VAT on goods and services bought as well as income tax on earnings.

The effect on business includes:

- A cut in income tax may give consumers more disposable income, thus raising consumption
- However, if income tax is raised this may discourage spending and reduce consumption
- A cut in corporation tax may increase available profits for businesses which may stimulate investment
- Changes to VAT will affect the price to consumers and also the costs to a business

## Changes in exchange rates

**Exchange rates** are the price of one currency in terms of another e.g. £1 = $1.50.

An increase in the value of a currency is called an **appreciation** this means the currency is worth more e.g. £1 = $1.60.

A decrease in the value of a currency is called a **depreciation** this means the currency is worth less e.g. £1 = $1.40.

> If a pair of trainers costs £50 in the UK and are exported to USA, assuming the exchange rates is £1: $1.50, they would cost $75.
>
> £50 x £1.50 = **$75**

The effect on businesses:

- SPICED (strong pound: imports cheaper, exports dearer)
    - Firms that import will be able to buy cheaper raw materials and finished goods
    - Firms that export will see less demand
- WPIDEC (weak pound: imports dearer, exports cheaper)
    - There will be greater demand from abroad for UK goods
    - Input prices will increase if raw materials are imported
    - If the firm has a price inelastic product it will be able to pass the increase in costs onto the consumer
- Fluctuations in exchange rates create uncertainties
    - Prices will change regularly if a firm trades with foreign businesses
- This will impact on the competitiveness of businesses, with costs and revenues increasing or decreasing and the profitability of the business being affected favourably or adversely

# Test Yourself

## 1.5.4 The economy and business

1. What are interest rates?

2. Explain how a rise in interest rates might affect a business that relies on loans.

3. Explain how a fall in interest rates might affect consumers.

4. What is employment?

5. Explain one positive affect of a rise in employment levels on a business.

6. Explain one negative affect of a rise in employment levels on a business.

7. What is consumer income?

8. Explain what will happen to demand for luxury goods if income levels rise.

9. What are exchange rates?

10. What is Government taxation?

## 1.5.5 External influences

**What you need to learn**
- The importance of external influences on business:
  - possible responses by the business to changes in: technology, legislation, the economic climate

Businesses will respond in a number of ways to changes in **technology**:

### Increased investment
- High initial investment to buy and install new equipment
- Looking at different methods of raising finance due to additional costs
- This could lead to long term cost savings and less waste

### Innovation
- New product or processes giving a unique selling point to the business
- New opportunities for products taking advantage of new technologies
- New innovative routes to market, such as through e-commerce
- Heavy investment in research and development

### Marketing
- Greater use of e-commerce to target markets
- New media opportunities
- New ways of communicating with customers e.g. blogs, reviews and company websites

**Employment**
- New opportunities
  - Training
  - Innovative culture
  - Business technology start-ups
- However, there are threats
  - Monotonous jobs or the loss of skills
  - Redundancies
  - Out of date skills

Businesses continually have to deal with changes in **legislation**. These occur regularly as the UK Government enacts new laws. As the Government changes regularly so does the law.

Businesses will have to set aside resources to meet changes in the law:

- Human Resource Management (HRM) will have to ensure that employees are recruited appropriately e.g. no discrimination and that employees are paid according to the law e.g. minimum wage and are trained properly e.g. health and safety
- Operations management will need to ensure equipment is kept up-to-date and maintained appropriately
- Finance will have to ensure that financial resources are available for the business in order to meet the cost of the new legislation
- Marketing will need to ensure that all areas e.g. pricing and product quality meet the legal requirements

Failure to meet new legislation requirements could lead to significant costs in terms of financial penalties and to the reputation of the business. This could ultimately lead to lower sales or even business failure.

Businesses continually have to deal with changes to the **economic climate**. As these are external influences the business might undertake market research to inform it as to how changes might impact both positively and negatively.

A business might respond to the following changes:
- Increased **unemployment** will lead to lower demand in the economy. Businesses might seek to lower costs by reducing the size of the workforce and putting pressure on suppliers to lower their prices. This might lead to a range of lower priced products
- If **consumer incomes** rise they are more able to purchase better quality goods and services. Business might develop new products in order to meet increased demand. They can also raise prices as consumers have higher disposable incomes
- **Inflation** will increase costs for a business. If there is a lack of substitutes or no close competitors the business might pass these costs on to the consumer. If there is plenty of competition the business might have to absorb the costs and face lower profit margins
- Higher **interest rates** will lead to lower demand in the economy. This will particularly impact on those products purchased through loans such as cars and houses. These businesses might respond by reducing the amount of stock that they hold, minimising their own holding costs and reducing the likelihood of unsold stock
- Increased **government taxation** will lead to less disposable income. Demand will fall and businesses might look to offer a cheaper range of goods and services
- A depreciation of the **exchange rate** will increase the cost of imports. Businesses that import their products will try to increase price or absorb the increased cost, impacting on profits. Alternatively, they might look for new suppliers, particularly domestically. Exporters will have to gear up for an increase in demand as exports become cheaper. They are likely to take on new staff and employ more resources to meet this extra demand

# Test Yourself

## 1.5.5 External influences

1. What is meant by external influences?

2. Explain one impact of technology on marketing.

3. Explain one impact of technology on operations.

4. What is meant by legislation?

5. Explain one impact of legislation on human resources.

6. Explain one impact of legislation on finance.

7. Explain one impact on a business of an increase in government taxation.

8. Explain one impact on a business of an increase in the value of the £.

9. Explain one possible response by a business to changes in technology.

10. Explain one possible response by a business to changes in the economic climate.